LIGHT IN THE WILDERNESS

LIGHT IN THE WILDERNESS

Paul von Baich

Toronto
OXFORD UNIVERSITY PRESS
1981

Passages from the King James Version
of the Psalms and the Book of Isaiah
selected and arranged by Roger Boulton.

ISBN 0-19-540374-6

2 3 4 - 4 3

Printed in Hong Kong by
EVERBEST PRINTING COMPANY LIMITED

Wilderness was a recurrent setting for revelation throughout the Bible. To the ancient Hebrews it was the natural theatre in which history was enacted as a dialogue between God and man. In the wilderness man was guided, tested, inspired, and granted the knowledge that took him beyond his individual self to encounter the divine.

God's wilderness is not confined in time or space. Always, in any wilderness, man may find him. The photographs in this book were taken on several journeys in the Yukon and the Northwest Territories of Canada. They were taken with no conscious religious thoughts in mind. This very unselfconsciousness bears witness to the spiritual nature of the experiences they record. Paul von Baich and Robert Frisch were simply exploring a country they had come to know well over the years. As they canoed and portaged, backpacked on the mountains, and struggled through the snow, Paul von Baich photographed the sights around him with the wonder and appreciation of an artist.

A year ago we were talking at his home in Campbellford, Ontario, about how, if at all, we might present these photographs in a book. What was their meaning? They seemed to have some significance beyond the obvious beauty of the landscapes as such. I remarked to Paul that whenever he spoke of the wilderness he used the language of pilgrimage, words like 'renewal', 'purity', 'searching', words that implied much more than simply exploration for adventure's sake. I asked him if we might try to match the photographs with sentences from the Psalms, to make a composite prayer of thanksgiving and hope. This book is the result.

ROGER BOULTON
Toronto, 1981

List of plates

1 In the Ogilvie Mountains, Yukon, at approximately 65°N, 138°W. We called this 'Castle Mountain', but I have never found it marked on any map.

2 A west wind is driving cirrus clouds above the Bonnet Plume River, Yukon. This river rises in the Mackenzie Mountains and flows north north-west to join the Peel River which in turn flows into the Mackenzie River and so to the Arctic Ocean.

3 Rainstorm on 'Castle Mountain'.

4 In the darkness of winter, the aurora borealis flares above the forests of the Yukon River.

5 Light and dark and storm again, with a rainbow over 'Castle Mountain'.

6 On a summer evening the sunlight moves up a nameless hillside, leaving the gravel beds of the Bonnet Plume to the night.

7 Robert Frisch, my wilderness companion, a veteran traveller of the North.

8 Morning mist in the forests of the Bonnet Plume; it lasts only a moment, and then the mist is burned off by the sudden brilliance of the sun.

9 This part of the Ogilvies was never glaciated. It stood above the ice and its flower species survived the ice age; but the limestone is soft and erosion has carved these turrets and pillars. Every now and then the rock comes tinkling down, marking the passage of time.

10 After a week of rain there is dew on every branch. We are at Boundary Creek on the Alaska-Yukon border.

11 Bob is backpacking down a moose trail, from Boundary Creek to the Tatonduk River, a two-day march across a mountain divide.

12 Along the Camsell River, traversing another divide, the watershed between Great Slave Lake and Great Bear Lake in the Northwest Territories. Bob is in the stern of our two-man wood-and-canvas canoe.

13 Camp at Little Sit-Down Creek, Yukon; our tent is in the background, where we are smoking bearmeat.

14 Camp-fire on the Bonnet Plume.

15 Lichen will grow only in conditions of purity; you will never find it in polluted air or waters.

16 Morning in camp on the Bonnet Plume.

17 Evening sunlight flashes on the lakes of the Mackenzie Delta near Aklavik, Northwest Territories.

18 Morning cloud sweeping across the Ogilvies, just off the Dempster Highway north of Dawson City, Yukon.

19 Grouard Lake, one day's travel south of Great Bear Lake, at one o'clock in the morning, end of June.

20 Evening on Faber Lake, Northwest Territories; lots of mosquitoes.

21 Five-Finger Rapids, Yukon River, in September.

22 Midnight in July on the Yukon River.

23 Evening on Kluane Lake, Yukon.

24 Northern Ogilvies from the air, between Old Crow and Dawson City.

25 Sunlight on trembling aspens, below the Ogilvies.

26 Fording the Tatonduk River.

27 Spring run-off; after the snow comes a waterfall that lasts for only a couple of weeks.

28 Manoeuvering the canoe in shallow water, using a pole and two lines.

29 Autumn colour of the *Arctostaphylos rubra*, the Bearberry or Kinnickinick.

30 A break for lunch; the air and the light are pink from nearby forest fires.

31 Evening along the Alaska Highway, near Kluane National Park.

32 Rafting on the Yukon River; Bob and John Algotsson, who joined us for two weeks by raft on that part of the journey. On the raft we put a stove, kitchen equipment, everything we needed to eat and sleep aboard.

33 More limestone pillars, these in the Peel River Canyon, Yukon, just past the confluence of the Peel and the Bonnet Plume. The cliffs are studded with white spruce trees.

34 Overnight camp in the Bonnet Plume Canyon.

35 Tea-break on the Peel River.

36 Northern Ogilvies at the headwaters of the Porcupine River, in early October; well above the tree-line, the shrubbery still shows through the first light snowfall.

37 Breaking trail for the dog-team on a side-arm of the Yukon River.

38 'Snowshoes,' Bob once said, 'let you step into magic. The magic is all about you and right underfoot.'

39 Last rest before camp; the remains of a tree-stump give us light and warmth on the trail.

40 Struggling with a blizzard on the Chilkoot Pass.

41 Climbing the 'Golden Stairs', the last stretch to the summit of the Chilkoot Pass.

42 Bivouac below the Chilkoot summit.

43 Chilkoot Pass.

44 Dusk on the Bonnet Plume.

45 First snow on the Ogilvies and fifty degrees of frost; early morning in October on the Dempster Highway.

46 *Anemone narcissiflora.*

47 Trail's end, a cabin near Dawson.

48 Haines Road, on the border between British Columbia and the Yukon.

PAUL VON BAICH

The heavens declare the glory of God

PSALM 19 v.1

And the firmament sheweth his handywork
PSALM 19 v.1

O send out thy light and thy truth

PSALM 43 v.3

Let them lead me
PSALM 43 v.3

Let them bring me unto thy holy hill

PSALM 43 v.3

For thou art my rock and my fortress
PSALM 71 v.3

Shew me thy ways, O Lord;
teach me thy paths
PSALM 25 v.4

Make me to go in the path of thy commandments;
for therein do I delight

PSALM 119 v.35

O Lord, how manifold are thy works!

PSALM 104 v.24

In wisdom thou hast made them all:
the earth is full of thy riches

PSALM 104 v. 24

My voice shalt thou hear in the morning, O Lord;
in the morning will I direct my prayer unto thee

PSALM 5 v.3

If I take the wings of the morning
PSALM 139 v.9

And dwell in the uttermost parts of the sea
PSALM 139 v.9

Even there shall thy hand lead me,
and thy right hand shall hold me

PSALM 139 v.10

When I consider thy heavens, the work of thy fingers,
the moon and the stars, which thou hast ordained;
What is man, that thou art mindful of him?
and the son of man, that thou visitest him?

PSALM 8 vv.3 & 4

Thy mercy, O Lord, is in the heavens;
and thy faithfulness reacheth unto the clouds.
Thy righteousness is like the great mountains;
thy judgements are a great deep

PSALM 36 vv. 5 & 6

Therefore the children of men put their trust under the shadow of thy wings

PSALM 36 v.7

Thou shalt make them drink of the river of thy pleasures.
For with thee is the fountain of life

PSALM 36 vv.8 & 9

Seek ye the Lord while he may be found

ISAIAH 55 v.6

Call ye upon him while he is near
ISAIAH 55 v.6

Commit thy way unto the Lord; trust also in him

PSALM 37 v.5

Rest in the Lord, and wait patiently for him

PSALM 37 v.7

Trust in the Lord, and do good;
so shalt thou dwell in the land
PSALM 37 v.3

And verily thou shalt be fed
PSALM 37 v.3

He that dwelleth in the secret place of the most High

PSALM 91 v.1

Shall abide under the shadow of the Almighty

PSALM 91 v.1

The Lord is my light and my salvation;
whom shall I fear?

PSALM 27 v.1

The Lord is the strength of my life;
of whom shall I be afraid?

PSALM 27 v.1

Lord, thou hast been our dwelling place in all generations. Before the mountains were brought forth, or ever thou hadst formed the earth and the world, even from everlasting to everlasting, thou art God

PSALM 90 vv.1 & 2

For a thousand years in thy sight are but as yesterday
when it is past, and as a watch in the night.
So teach us to number our days,
that we may apply our hearts unto wisdom

PSALM 90 vv.4 & 12

I will sing praise to my God while I have my being.
My meditation of him shall be sweet

PSALM 104 v v.33 & 34

And now, Lord, what wait I for?

PSALM 39 v.7

My hope is in thee

PSALM 39 v.7